Bible Boogie ABCs is a book/music learning program in the **Bible Boogie Series** that introduces children to scriptures from the Bible using upbeat music. This book includes a word, scripture, summary sentence, and song lyrics for every letter of the alphabet. The music, which can be purchased separately online, includes narrations of the scripture pages and songs for the lyrics in this book. There is a song for every letter of the alphabet as well as a dance-along opening song and closing ABC song. Look for dance-along videos on YouTube.

To hear snippets of the music or purchase entire songs, visit https://bibleboogieabcs.hearnow.com (website includes links to Spotify, Apple Music, iTunes, Amazon, Pandora, and Deezer).

Bible Boogie ABCs is a great spiritual tool for Sunday School, Bible Study, Chapel, devotional time, family time, travel time, and more!

Look for other books in the Bible Boogie Series soon:

- *Bible Boogie Colors*
- *Bible Boogie 123s*
- *Bible Boogie Shapes*

Copyright © 2021 by MEWE Music

Bible Boogie ABCs Lyrics and Music © 2021
All rights reserved. No part of this book or CD may be used or duplicated without written permission from the publisher. Scripture references are taken from the King James Version of the Bible.

Bible Boogie Series
bibleboogie.com

ISBN: 978-1-7360565-2-3

Library of Congress Control Number: 2021947010

For Worldwide Distribution
Printed in the USA

Contents

Letters, Scriptures, & Lyrics	4-55
Bible Boogie ABCs Dance-along Lyrics	56-57
Activity Page	58
Purchasing Information	59
Bible Boogie ABCs Summary	60

Adam

Genesis 2:20

And Adam gave names to all cattle, and to the fowl of the air, and to every beast of the field;

Adam was the first man God created.

# Adam Was the First

Adam was the first, Adam was the first,
Adam was the first man that God made
Adam was the first, Adam was the first,
Adam was the first man that God made

Adam named the animals,
Adam named the animals,
Adam named the animals that God made
Adam named the animals,
Adam named the animals,
Adam named the animals that God made

Repeat all

Adam was the first man that God made
Adam was the first man that God made
Adam was the first man that God made

Bethlehem

John 7:42

Hath not the scripture said, That Christ cometh of the seed of David, and out of the town of Bethlehem, where David was?

Bethlehem is the place where Jesus was born.

 Town Called Bethlehem

There is a town called Bethlehem
Where Jesus Christ was born
He laid down in a manger
As the wise men looked upon
The Savior who had come to earth
To save us all from sin

All praises to this Holy One
For we should worship Him
All praises to this Holy One
For we should worship Him

Repeat all

Child

Proverbs 22:6

Train up a child in the way he should go: and when he is old, he will not depart from it.

A child should be trained according to God's word.

Train Up a Child

Train up a child in the way he should go
He won't depart, when he gets old

Train up a child in the way he should go
He won't depart, when he gets old

He won't depart - when he gets old
He won't depart - when he gets old
He won't depart - when he gets old
Train up a child in the way he should go

Children obey your parents in the Lord
For this is right to do from the very start

Children obey your parents in the Lord
For this is right to do from the very start

For this is right to do from the very start
For this is right to do from the very start
For this is right to do from the very start
Children obey - your parents in the Lord

Train up a child
Train up a child

I Samuel 17:50

So David prevailed over the Philistine with a sling and with a stone, and smote the Philistine, and slew him; but there was no sword in the hand of David.

David defeated Goliath with a sling and a stone.

David the Shepherd Boy

David - the shepherd boy who was brave
David - the shepherd boy who was brave
David - the shepherd boy who was brave
David - the shepherd boy who was brave

His brothers laughed at him
When he decided to go
Fight the Giant called Goliath
'Cause the others said NO

David slew Goliath
With a sling and a stone
He didn't have an army
He fought on his own

Repeat all

David - the shepherd boy who was brave
David - the shepherd boy who was brave
David - the shepherd boy who was brave
David - the shepherd boy who was brave

Eve

Genesis 3:20

And Adam called his wife's name Eve; because she was the mother of all living.

Eve was the first woman God created.

Mother of All Living

The mother of all living
God took a rib from a man
The mother of all living
The Bible calls her Eve

The mother of all living
God took a rib from a man
The mother of all living
The Bible calls her Eve

(Rap)
Genesis 2:22, the Bible tells us that
Eve was the first woman God made -
That's a fact
She was formed using a rib taken from a man
Who was alone in this world
And needed a friend

Repeat all

The mother of all living
The Bible calls her Eve!

Faith

Mark 11:22

And Jesus answering saith unto them, Have faith in God.

Jesus wants us to have faith in God.

We Walk by Faith

We walk by faith and not by sight
We walk by faith and not by sight
We walk by faith and not by sight
We walk by faith and not by sight
Trusting in His Holy Word
And seeking all His kingdom first

Repeat all

We walk by faith and not by sight
We walk by faith and not by sight
We walk by faith and not by sight
We walk by faith

God

Genesis 1:1

In the beginning God created the heaven and the earth.

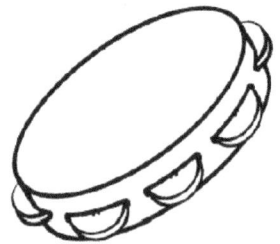

God is the Creator of all things.

# He Made It All

The sun - God made it
The moon - God made it
The stars - God made it
He made it all

The sun - God made it
The moon - God made it
The stars - God made it
He made it all

He made the heavens
He made the earth
And all that dwells within
All that is beautiful
All that is wonderful
Yes God He made them

Repeat all

The sun - God made it
The moon - God made it
The stars - God made it
He made it all

Hannah

I Samuel 1:20

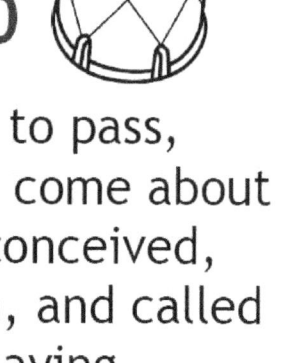

Wherefore it came to pass, when the time was come about after Hannah had conceived, that she bare a son, and called his name Samuel, saying, Because I have asked him of the Lord.

Hannah prayed for a son and God answered her prayer.

Hannah's Prayer

Hannah wept because she wanted a son
Hannah wept because she wanted a son
Hannah wept because she wanted a son
So she went to God in prayer

Hannah prayed and God delivered a son
Hannah prayed and God delivered a son
Hannah prayed and God delivered a son
Because she prayed to God in faith

Repeat all

Hannah wept because she wanted a son
Hannah wept because she wanted a son
Hannah wept because she wanted a son
So she went to God in prayer

Instruments

Psalm 150:4

Praise him with the timbrel and dance: praise him with stringed instruments and organs.

God wants us to praise him with instruments.

 # Instrument Praise

Can you hear the trumpet?
Can you hear the tambourine?
Can you hear the lute, the harp,
The flute, the cymbals clashing

Can you hear the trumpet?
Can you hear the tambourine?
Can you hear the instruments PRAISE
Our risen King

Repeat all

Repeat all

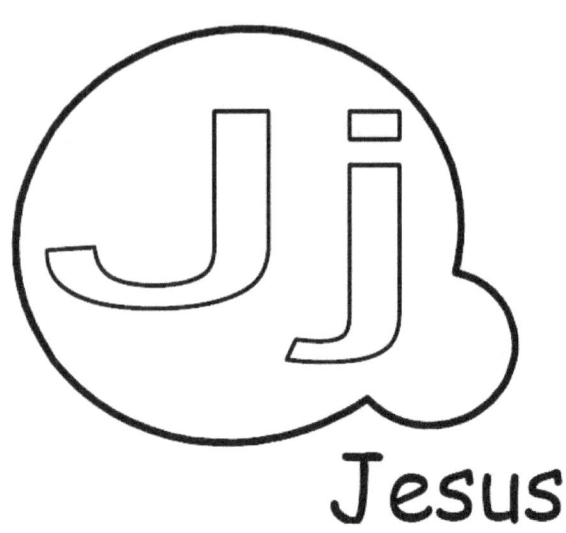

Jesus

Matthew 1:21

And she shall bring forth a son, and thou shalt call his name JESUS: for he shall save his people from their sins.

Jesus is the Son of God.

Son of God

Jesus, Jesus, Jesus is the Son of God
Jesus, Jesus, Jesus is the Son of God

Holy, Holy, Holy is the Son of God
Holy, Holy, Holy is the Son of God

Righteous, Righteous, Righteous is the Son of God
Righteous, Righteous, Righteous is the Son of God

Jesus, Jesus, Jesus is the Son of God
Jesus, Jesus, Jesus is the Son of God

Jesus, Jesus, Jesus is the Son of God
Jesus, Jesus, Jesus is the Son of God

Jesus, Jesus, Jesus is the Son of God
Jesus, Jesus, Jesus is the Son of God

Kk

Kneel

Psalm 95:6

O come, let us worship and bow down: let us kneel before the Lord our maker.

Sometimes we kneel in God's presence during worship.

 # Kneel Down to Pray

When we kneel down to pray
We thank the Lord for one more day

When we kneel down to pray
We thank the Lord for one more day

When we kneel down to pray
We thank the Lord for one more day

When we kneel and bow our heads
to pray
We thank the Lord for one more day

Repeat all

Repeat all

Love

I John 4:7

Beloved, let us love one another: for love is of God; and every one that loveth is born of God, and knoweth God.

God wants us to love one another.

God Is Love

   L   O   V   E   God is love
   L   O   V   E   God is love
   L   O   V   E   God is love
   L   O   V   E   God is love

Love each other as He loves us
We know in God in whom we trust
If we can love a God we can't see
Then we can love each other certainly

Repeat all

   L   O   V   E   God is love
   L   O   V   E   God is love
   L   O   V   E   God is love
   L   O   V   E   God is love

Love each other as He loves us
We know in God in whom we trust

Mary

Luke 1:38

And Mary said, Behold the handmaid of the Lord; be it unto me according to thy word. And the angel departed from her.

Mary was the mother of Jesus.

Mary, Mary

The angel came to Mary
And said you will have a Son
Because you're highly favored -
Don't you fear that you're the one
Mary told the angel
Be it unto me
I will have the Savior
Who will set the people free

Mary, Mary thank you for
Having the baby
Mary, Mary Jesus saved both
You and me
Jesus saved both you and me

Repeat all

Mary, Mary thank you for having the baby

Noah

Genesis 7:1

And the Lord said unto Noah, Come thou and all thy house into the ark; for thee have I seen righteous before me in this generation.

God told Noah to build an ark.

Come on into the Ark

Our God told Noah to build an ark
Come on inside before the rain starts
Righteousness He sees in you from above
He will protect you from the flood

Come on into the ark
Bring the animals with you
Come on into the ark
Two by two
Come on into the ark
Bring your wife and children
Come on into the ark
Before the flood begins

Repeat all

Offering

Exodus 25:2

Speak unto the children of Israel, that they bring me an offering: of every man that giveth it willingly with his heart ye shall take my offering.

We should willingly give offerings to God.

Offering of Thanks

With a willing heart give unto God
An offering of thanks
With a willing heart give unto God
An offering of thanks
With a willing heart give unto God
An offering of thanks

Give unto Him, He is worthy
Give unto Him, He is worthy
Give unto Him an offering, an offering,
An offering of thanks

Repeat all (With a sincere heart)

With a willing heart give unto God
An offering of thanks
With a willing heart give unto God
An offering of thanks
With a willing heart give unto God
An offering of thanks

Give unto Him, He is worthy
Give unto Him, He is worthy

Prayer

Matthew 21:22

And all things, whatsoever ye shall ask in prayer, believing, ye shall receive.

We communicate with God through prayer.

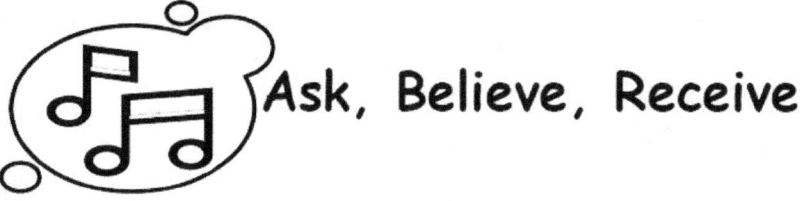 Ask, Believe, Receive

Ask, believe, receive
Ask, believe, receive
Whatever you want
Go to God in prayer and
Ask, believe, receive

Repeat

Ask Him with boldness
Believe in your heart
Receive His many blessings
From the very start

Repeat all

Ask, believe, receive
Ask, believe, receive
Whatever you want
Go to God in prayer and
Ask, believe, receive

Repeat

Queen Esther

Esther 7:3

Then Esther the Queen answered and said, If I have found favour in thy sight, O king, and if it please the king, let my life be given me at my petition, and my people at my request:

Queen Esther went before the King on behalf of the people.

Oh King

King, if it pleases thee, Oh king
Would you give me my life
And the lives of all the people
Who are dear to me

Oh king, Esther went before the king
She found favor with king
Who gave her everything
She boldly asked of him

Oh king, Jesus Is the King
Let us go before the King
He will give you everything
That you desire

Oh king, Jesus Is the King
Let us go before the King
He will give you everything
That you desire
Oh King

Repeat all

Red Sea

Acts 7:36

He [Moses] brought them out, after that he had shewed wonders and signs in the land of Egypt, and in the Red sea, and in the wilderness forty years.

The children of Israel crossed the Red Sea after leaving Egypt.

Walk on Over

The children of Israel left Egypt land
Followed Moses with a rod in his hand
Approached the Red Sea
And were scared that day
But then Moses heard God say

Stretch out your rod and
Watch the water divide
Walk on over to the other side
Don't you worry 'bout your enemies
They won't make it cross the Red Sea

Walk on over, walk, walk
Walk on over, walk, walk
Walk on over to the other side
Walk on over to the other side

Stretch out your rod and
Watch the water divide
Walk on over to the other side

Sanctuary

Psalm 134:2

Lift up your hands in the sanctuary, and bless the Lord.

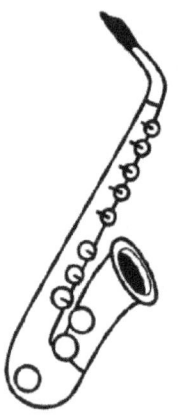

The sanctuary is a holy place of worship.

In the Sanctuary

Lift up your hands in the sanctuary
Lift up your hands
Come and bless the Lord with me
He is worthy to be praised
In the sanctuary
He is worthy to be praised
Come and bless the Lord with me

Lift up your voice in the sanctuary
Lift up your voice
Come and bless the Lord with me
He is worthy to be praised
In the sanctuary
He is worthy to be praised
Come and bless the Lord with me

In the sanctuary...in the sanctuary
In the sanctuary...in the sanctuary

Time

Ecclesiastes 3:4

A time to weep, and a time to laugh; a time to mourn, and a time to dance;

God has a time for everything.

It's Time to Dance

Time to dance before the Lord
Time to dance before the Lord
Time to dance before the Lord
It's time to dance

Lift your hands, stomp your feet
Give him praise for victory
Come on and dance before the Lord
Show forth His praises - rejoice

Repeat

Time to dance before the Lord
Time to dance before the Lord
Time to dance before the Lord
It's time to dance

Victory, Victory, Victory – I've Got It
Victory, Victory, Victory – I've Got It

Repeat (Time to dance...)

Get your praise on (repeat 4 times)

Unity

Psalm 133:1

Behold, how good and how pleasant it is for brethren to dwell together in unity!

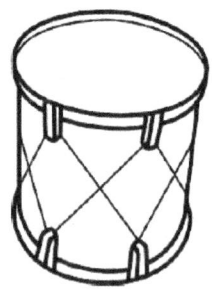

God wants his people to live in unity.

 # Together in Unity

Behold, how good and how pleasant it is
For brethren to dwell together in unity
Behold, how good and how pleasant it is
To dwell in unity

It's like the precious ointment on the head
That runs down on the beard
It's like the dew falling upon
The mountains of Zion

Behold, how good and how pleasant it is
For brethren to dwell together in unity
Behold, how good and how pleasant it is
To dwell in unity

Can we come together
Together in unity

It's good, It's good
Together in unity

Repeat (Behold, how good...)

Victory

Psalm 98:1

O sing unto the Lord a new song; for he hath done marvelous things: his right hand, and his holy arm, hath gotten him the victory.

We have the victory through Jesus Christ.

I Have Victory

I have the victory
Because of Calvary
My Jesus died for me
I'll live eternally

V I C T O R Y
I have the victory
V I C T O R Y
Because of Calvary
V I C T O R Y
My Jesus died for me

I have victory
Because of Calvary
My Jesus died for me
I'll live eternally

Worship

John 4:24

God is a Spirit: and they that worship him must worship him in spirit and in truth.

We can honor and adore God in worship.

 # In Spirit and Truth

Worship in spirit and truth
Worship in spirit and truth
God is a Spirit and they that worship Him
Must worship Him in spirit and truth
God is a Spirit and they that worship Him
Must worship Him in spirit and truth

Repeat all

Repeat all

In spirit and truth
In spirit and truth
In spirit and truth
In spirit and truth!

Excellent

I Corinthians 12:31

But covet earnestly the best gifts: and yet shew I unto you a more excellent way.

God wants us to show love – it is the more excellent way.

A More Excellent Way

There's a more excellent, excellent
There's a more excellent way
There's a more excellent, excellent
There's a more excellent way

Repeat

God is - God's a more excellent way
God is - God's a more excellent way

There's a more excellent way,
There's a more excellent way
There's a more excellent way,
There's a more excellent way

Love is - Love's a more excellent way
Love is - Love's a more excellent way

There's a more excellent way,
There's a more excellent way
There's a more excellent way,
There's a more excellent way

There's a more excellent, excellent
There's a more excellent way

Youth

Psalm 103:5

Who satisfieth thy mouth with good things; so that thy youth is renewed like the eagle's.

God gives us things that are good for us.

 Renew Your Youth

Renew your youth like an eagle
Renew your youth like an eagle
Renew your youth just like an eagle
Because of the good things you say

Repeat

Say that you love God
Say that you care
Say that you love
The people everywhere

Say that you trust God
Say that you give
Say that you walk according
To His perfect will

Repeat all

Repeat (Renew your youth...)

Zion

Psalm 48:2

Beautiful for situation, the joy of the whole earth, is mount Zion, on the sides of the north, the city of the great King.

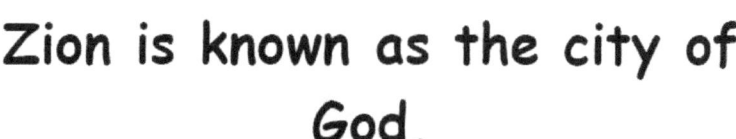

Zion is known as the city of God.

Let's Go Up to Zion

Let's go up to Zion
Let's go up to Zion
The Spirit of the Lord is calling
Let's go up to Zion

Let's go worship in Zion
Let's go worship in Zion
The Spirit of the Lord is calling
Let's go worship in Zion

Let's go pray in Zion
Let's go pray in Zion
The Spirit of the Lord is calling
Let's go pray in Zion

Let's go up to Zion
Let's go up to Zion
The Spirit of the Lord is calling
Let's go up to Zion

Let's go up to Zion
Let's go up to Zion
Let's go up to Zion

Bible Boogie ABCs Dance-along

Come sing with me Bible ABCs
Yeah, yeah, yeah
Come sing with me Bible ABCs
Yeah, yeah, yeah

We're going through the Bible
We'll start with letter A
We're going through the Bible
We will lead the way

We're going through the Bible
This journey has begun
We're going through the Bible
Learning can be fun

Clap your hands
Stomp your feet
Turn around
Twist your knees

Walk it up
Now walk it back
Wave your arms
Just like that

Slide to the left
Slide to the right
Roll it out
Jump to the sky

Nod your head
Touch the ground
Reach up and snap
Now bounce

Robot freeze - Robot freeze
Robot freeze - Robot freeze

Now do your own thing - Do your own thing
Do your own thing - Do your own thing

Don't you know you're doing the
Bible Bible boogie now

Don't you know you're doing the
Bible boogie

Come sing with me Bible ABCs
Yeah, yeah, yeah
Come sing with me Bible ABCs
Yeah, yeah, yeah

Activity Page

Circle the tambourine.

Circle the guitar.

Visit www.bibleboogie.com for more activities and events.

Purchasing Information

To purchase Bible Boogie ABCs music, visit:
- https://bibleboogieabcs.hearnow.com

Note: The website includes links to Spotify, Apple Music, iTunes, Amazon, Pandora, and Deezer.

To purchase more copies of the Bible Boogie ABCs book or other books available in the Bible Boogie Series, visit:
- www.bibleboogie.com
- Amazon.com (keywords: Bible Boogie)
- BarnesandNobles.com (keywords: Bible Boogie)

To purchase merchandise for the Bible Boogie Series, visit:
- www.bibleboogie.com

To contact us about upcoming events or new releases in the Bible Boogie Series, visit:
- www.bibleboogie.com

Look for these and other releases in the Bible Boogie Series soon:

- *Bible Boogie Colors*
- *Bible Boogie 123s*
- *Bible Boogie Shapes*

Bible Boogie ABCs Summary

A – Adam
B – Bethlehem
C – Child
D – David
E – Eve
F – Faith
G – God
H – Hannah
I – Instruments
J – Jesus
K – Kneel
L – Love
M – Mary

N – Noah
O – Offering
P – Prayer
Q – Queen Esther
R – Red Sea
S – Sanctuary
T – Time
U – Unity
V – Victory
W – Worship
X – eXcellent
Y – Youth
Z – Zion

A B C D E F G H I J K L M
N O P Q R S T U V W X Y Z

www.ingramcontent.com/pod-product-compliance
Lightning Source LLC
Chambersburg PA
CBHW062202100526
44589CB00014B/1917